The Supreme Court

The Supreme Court

Brendan January

Franklin Watts
A Division of Scholastic Inc.
New York • Toronto • London • Auckland • Sydney
Mexico City • New Delhi • Hong Kong
Danbury, Connecticut

Note to readers: Definitions for words in **bold** can be found in the Glossary at the back of this book.

The illustration on the cover shows justices of the Supreme Court. The photograph opposite the title page shows the Supreme Court building.

Photographs © 2004: AP/Wide World Photos: 48 (Charles Rex Arbogast), 30, 36; Art Resource, NY: 20, 22 (National Portrait Gallery, Smithsonian Institution, Washington, DC), 14 (Private Collection); Corbis Images: 10, 25, 28, 37, 44 bottom (Bettmann), 34, 44 top; Folio, Inc.: 2 (Walter Bibikow), 5 top, 12 (Fred J. Maroon); Getty Images: 6 (Carl Iwasaki), 51 (Mark Wilson); Library of Congress: 32; Missouri Historical Society, St. Louis, MO: 29; North Wind Picture Archives: 19, 26; PhotoEdit: 38; Photri Inc.: 17, 23; Supreme Court Historical Society/Richard Strauss/Smithsonian Institution: cover; Supreme Court of the United States, Office of the Curator/Franz Jantzen: 5 bottom, 46; The Image Works/Rob Crandall: 49; Time Life Pictures/Getty Images: 40 (Esther Bubley), 35 (John Loengard), 43.

Library of Congress Cataloging-in-Publication Data

January, Brendan.
    The Supreme Court / Brendan January.
        p. cm. — (Watts library)
    Includes bibliographical references and index.
    ISBN 0-531-12294-8 (lib. bdg.)   0-531-16384-9 (pbk.)
    1. United States. Supreme Court—History—Juvenile literature. 2. Courts of last resort—United States—Juvenile literature. 3. Judicial process—United States—Juvenile literature. I. Title. II. Series.
KF8742.Z9J36 2004
347.73'26—dc22

                                                                                            2004002008

Contents

Linda Brown's parents sued the Topeka Board of Education because Linda (front and center) was forced to travel to an all-black school.

Chapter One

A Fateful Decision

At noon on May 17, 1954, nine judges dressed in flowing black robes entered a large chamber in the Supreme Court. They quietly took their seats behind a long wooden table at the head of the hall. Behind the judges towered four marble columns and a curtain of scarlet. In front of them, the courtroom was packed with listeners and journalists, who sat in hushed excitement. The judges, it was announced, had **unanimously** decided a case called *Brown* v. *Board of Education*.

Oliver Brown was an African-American who lived in Topeka, Kansas. Brown became part of a **lawsuit** against the Topeka Board of Education because his eight-year-old daughter, Linda, couldn't attend a school nearby their home. The school was for white students only. Instead, Linda had to travel across town to a school for black students.

Brown's case, however, was about more than just Linda. It challenged **segregation**, a system of laws that separated white people and black people in public places. Segregation was especially common in the southern states. Black and white people went to separate schools. They sat in divided sections on buses and trains and in restaurants. Even the water fountains were segregated. Signs, such as "white only," told people where they could or could not drink.

Many southern whites argued that segregation was not bad, because it promised "separate but equal" treatment to both black and white Americans. In reality, however, segregation was not equal. In many parts of the country, African-Americans were forced to ride in filthy train cars, sit at the back of the bus, and attend crumbling schools without textbooks. Everyday, segregation reminded African-Americans that they were not valued in American society. Martin Luther King Jr., the civil rights activist, remembered eating in a railroad car where the waiter drew a curtain between him and the white diners. "I felt as if a curtain had been dropped on my selfhood," he recalled.

Brown's case was heard before the Supreme Court, where

his lawyers told the justices that the system of segregation was against the law. It had no place in a country that believed "all men are created equal." The justices listened carefully. The Supreme Court is the highest court in the land, and its decision is final.

Court Says No to Separate but Equal

In 1954, the Supreme Court decided against earlier "separate but equal" rulings. In a firm voice, Chief Justice Earl Warren announced that "'separate but equal' has no place" in the country's schools. "Separate educational facilities are inherently unequal," said Warren.

"To separate [African-American students] from others of similar age and qualifications solely because of their race," he continued, "generates a feeling of inferiority as to their status in the community that may affect their hearts and minds in a way unlikely ever to be undone."

There are few examples of a more powerful statement from the Supreme Court. One of the justices told a clerk, "if it was not the most important decision in the history of the Court, it was very close."

In the almost twenty minutes it took to read the opinion, the Court had delivered a crushing blow to segregation. The decision drew commentary from around the world and promised to change American society. For African-Americans and their supporters, it was a moment of triumph and hope.

"[The decision] will serve to close an ancient wound too

Chief Justice Earl Warren, pictured here, announced the Supreme Court decision declaring school segregation illegal.

long allowed to fester," wrote the *Post and Times Herald* in Washington, D.C. "It will bring to an end a painful disparity between American principles and American practices. It will help to refurbish American prestige in a world which looks to this land for moral inspiration and restore the faith of Americans themselves in their own great values and traditions."

Many white southerners felt a mixture of rage and disappointment. Some promised to resist. "The decision tortured the Constitution," said one southern politician. "The South will torture the decision."

A Special Role

What is the Supreme Court? How does it wield so much power in the United States? The answers to these questions are part of a fascinating story. It begins in the second half of the 1700s, when the thirteen colonies broke free of British rule and created a nation of their own, the United States of America. This nation was founded on the idea that each citizen has rights under the law. These rights must be protected by the judicial, or court, system.

No one was certain, however, how these rights would become a part of American life. Many were also unsure whether everyone, including African-Americans, women, and immigrants, should also enjoy these rights. These were questions that would take centuries to answer, and it was often the Supreme Court that answered them.

The current Supreme Court building was completed in 1935 for a cost of more than $9 million.

Chapter Two

The Highest Court

Today, the Supreme Court decides some of the most important cases in the United States. Each case is different, but they all raise questions about the role of government and the law in American life. The Court, for example, does much more than determine whether a citizen should pay a parking ticket, or how long a person must stay in jail for committing a serious crime. Other courts usually settle these issues, which arise all the time in communities across the nation. Rather, the Supreme Court hears cases about the power of government and the rights of citizens and groups.

Within the past two hundred years, the Court has ruled that a student does not have to recite the pledge of allegiance. The Court decided that a newspaper is free to publish almost anything about a public figure. It also determined that no U.S. citizen can be kept out of a public school because they are a man or a woman, black or white. It has decided that reciting a prayer over a loudspeaker before a high school football game is illegal. Recently, the Court has ruled on challenges made by George W. Bush and Al Gore in the 2000 presidential election.

The Court's role in American life began in the summer of 1787, when a group of Americans gathered in Philadelphia to debate and organize a new national government. This meet-

Members of the Constitutional Convention agreed that the government of the United States would have three branches: the executive, the legislative, and the judicial.

ing has been called the **Constitutional Convention**. The delegates, today called the "founders," agreed to create a strong Congress and president. They also established a branch of government made up of courts called the judicial branch, or the **judiciary**. In late August, they established a "supreme Court" in Article III of the Constitution. The Supreme Court was charged with having the final say about laws passed by Congress, legal arguments between states, and legal arguments between citizens from different states.

The justices are appointed to their position by the president and are approved by the Senate. The founders wanted judges to be free of the passion and deal-making common in politics. They serve on the Court until they die or choose to retire.

In 1789, Congress passed the Judiciary Act. The act created a Supreme Court of six judges with one chief justice and five associate justices. It also established two lower levels of courts. One level was made up of three circuit courts, each responsible for a region of the country: Eastern, Middle, and Southern. Below the circuit courts were thirteen district courts, one in each state.

There were, and are still today, separate systems of state courts. Each state has its own laws and courts to enforce them, and each state has a supreme court of its own. Only the U.S. Supreme Court can overrule a decision by a state supreme court. In the 1830s, the number of Supreme Court justices was expanded to nine.

Checks and Balances

The Constitution divided the federal government into three branches. They are the executive branch, the legislative branch, and the judicial branch. Why are there three branches? Each has a role in governing the nation, and the Constitution was written to keep any one branch from growing too strong. The Americans bitterly remembered how British rulers had disregarded the rights of American colonists. To prevent this from happening again, the Constitution gave each branch rights over the other branch through a system called **checks and balances**.

Establishing the Court

In 1790, the Supreme Court held its first session in New York City, then the nation's capital. Both the Constitution and the courts were brand new, and no one was certain what role the Court would play in American society. New Yorker Alexander Hamilton believed the Court would be weak because it had no money or soldiers. French visitor Alexis de Tocqueville, however, recognized the Court's power.

"I am unaware that any nation of the globe has organized a judicial power in the same manner as the Americans," de Tocqueville wrote. "A more imposing judicial power was never constituted by any people."

De Tocqueville was right. The justices, after all, were not voted into their positions. They were appointed for life. Both the president and the Congress had to listen to the voters and find solutions to the country's problems. If they did not, they would be quickly replaced. Justices on the Supreme Court, however, never had to face elections. They could make legal decisions based on what they believed the law meant without having to deal with political pressure.

It was not, however, that simple. Many justices paid close attention to what people thought, because the justices couldn't just order the nation to obey a law. The Court had to explain its position and justify its decision. If most citizens disagreed, the Court might lose its authority.

For this reason, the first justices were very careful. Many questions had to be answered for the first time. There was

The first Supreme Court justices were (top row, from left to right) John Jay (chief justice), James Iredell, John Blair, (bottom row, from left to right) William Cushing, James Wilson, and John Rutledge.

In the Constitution, there is a group of amendments known as the Bill of Rights. The Bill of Rights was first written to protect U.S. citizens from the actions of the federal government. Through these first ten amendments, individual citizens and states were guaranteed various freedoms, including the right to free speech, press, religion, and the protection of the law. Over the years, many amendments have been added to the Constitution. Today, there are twenty-seven! The Supreme Court often makes its decisions based on the protections listed in these amendments.

even a debate about how the justices would dress. Admirers of the English courts urged American judges to dress like English judges, complete with white powdered wig and dark robe.

Not everyone agreed. "For heaven's sake, discard the monstrous wig!" said Thomas Jefferson. One judge, William Cushing, wore a wig to the Court's first session. As he walked through the streets, a crowd of curious boys followed him. One supposedly remarked, "My eye! What a wig!" Humiliated, Cushing never wore a wig again.

The judges did, however, wear robes of black and red at their first meeting. They sat in a row at a table in the front of a chamber. An observer was impressed with the justices' "elegance, gravity, and neatness."

The Court, however, had little to do during its first few years. The Court was supposed to hear cases that were first decided in the district courts. When a case was decided, the parties had the right to ask a higher court to hear the case again. This is called an **appeal**. After the middle-level court's decision, the case can be appealed again. This time, it reaches the Supreme Court. It took a long time for decisions to be heard, appealed, and heard again. So the justices mostly sat and waited.

An Important Appointment

Because the Supreme Court still seemed unimportant during the 1790s, George Washington, the first president, found it difficult to attract well-qualified candidates. When the U.S.

government moved to Washington, D.C., it forgot to find a spot for the Court. A cramped and inconvenient chamber was finally located beneath the House of Representatives. There wasn't even a separate room for the judges to put on their robes.

In 1800, President John Adams offered the position of chief justice to several men, but they all turned it down. Finally, a friend and Virginian named John Marshall accepted. Marshall took his seat in 1801 and served until his death in 1835.

Chief Justice John Marshall served on the court for more than thirty years.

When Marshall became chief justice, the Court was still weak and unsure of its role in American government. Through his extraordinary vision and leadership, the Supreme Court was transformed. By 1835, the Court had become a major part of the government and the protector of the Constitution. It was a power respected by America's leaders and people.

During his final months in office, John Adams appointed members of his political party, the Federalists, to newly created positions.

Chapter Three

The Marshall Court

When John Marshall became chief justice of the Supreme Court, the nation was deeply divided. President John Adams, a member of the Federalist Party, had just been voted out of power. Adams was to be replaced by Thomas Jefferson, the leader of the Democrat-Republican Party. The Federalists and the Republicans bitterly disagreed on many issues.

In the months before Adams left the White House, the Federalists in Congress passed another judiciary act. Under this law, Adams appointed several Federalists to new federal court positions. The Republicans angrily claimed that the act had been passed just to benefit the Federalists. When Jefferson took power, his new secretary of state, James Madison, refused to deliver the papers that would confirm one of Adams's appointments, a man named William Marbury. Marbury sued Madison, saying that Madison must deliver the papers. Marbury argued that under the new judiciary act, his case should go directly to Marshall's Supreme Court. *Marbury* v. *Madison* would become one of the most important cases in U.S. history.

James Madison, Jefferson's secretary of state, refused to deliver the necessary paperwork to make William Marbury's appointment official.

Judicial Review

Marshall pondered the case. He could order Madison to deliver the papers. The Court, however, had no power to enforce its order. Madison might ignore the Court's decision, severely damaging the Court's standing. Or, Marshall could claim that the Supreme Court did not have the right to rule on the issue in the first place. Again, the Court would appear weak. Neither choice appeared good.

Instead, Marshall selected a third option. In his decision, Marshall said that the Judiciary Act did not agree with the Constitution. When Congress passed the act, it gave the Supreme Court powers beyond what the Constitution allowed. This was wrong, said Marshall. Congress did not have the right to give or take power from the Supreme Court. The Supreme Court's powers were established in the Constitution. No branch of government could change that. The Judiciary Act of 1801, wrote Marshall, was **unconstitutional**.

This decision was an enormous victory for the Supreme Court. Marshall's opinion struck down an act of Congress, setting an important example. From then on, the Supreme Court could judge whether laws passed by Congress agreed with the Constitution. This process is called "judicial review."

William Marbury sued James Madison and took his case to the Supreme Court.

Marshall's Method

During his thirty-four years on the Court, Marshall made several important decisions. It wasn't, however, just the decisions themselves that established Marshall's reputation. It was how Marshall made them. The Supreme Court announced its decisions in **opinions** that were written by one or more justices and read from the Court.

These opinions are crucial because they establish a **precedent**. Judges throughout the country use Court opinions to decide their own cases. If an opinion was confusing or poorly written, it raises more questions for these judges.

Marshall, however, wrote excellent opinions. He carefully argued his points, listed facts, and helped the reader to understand his conclusion. More often than not, the reader couldn't help but agree with Marshall.

Marshall also persuaded the other justices to support his opinion. This was also important. Even today the justices often argue among themselves about decisions. They take a vote and the position with the most votes, called the **majority**, becomes the decision of the Court. That's why Court decisions are announced with a number, such as "5-4" or "7-2." The justices who disagree can write a **dissenting opinion** that challenges the Court's reasoning.

McCulloch v. *Maryland*

This 1819 case raised the question of federal power versus state power. The U.S. Supreme Court decided that the federal government had the right to establish a national bank office in any state, and the state could not tax federal institutions.

During his time as chief justice, John Marshall helped strengthen the power of the Supreme Court.

Marshall, however, recognized that dissenting opinions made the Court look indecisive and weak. He worked hard to get the justices to agree to a single position. When a decision was reached, Marshall alone read the opinion of the Court.

Today, we name courts after the presiding chief justice. In Marshall's case, it was truly the Marshall Court. By the time Marshall died in 1835, his strong opinions had established the Court as an important power in the U.S. government.

"My gift of John Marshall to the people of the United States was the proudest act of my life," said John Adams.

As settlers established farms and settled in new territories in the West, there was much debate regarding whether slavery would be legal in these new regions.

Chapter Four

Civil Rights

After 1835, the United States experienced remarkable population growth. Immigrants, mostly from Europe, crowded into the cities along the east coast. White settlers, looking for land, eagerly moved west. The settlers divided the land into farms and planted crops. In the southern states, hundreds of thousands of black slaves worked on giant plantations.

In the northern states, many people objected to slavery, considering it cruel and inhumane. They argued that slavery should be ended, or **abolished**. Southerners reacted angrily to this criticism.

The tensions between proslavery and antislavery groups exploded into violence as both groups fought for control.

Slavery was the basis of the southern **agricultural** economy and the southern way of life.

The question of slavery, however, would not go away. White farmers in the north wanted the unsettled territories in the West reserved for them, not for slave owners. This angered southerners. They argued that slaves were property, like a horse or a plow, and were protected by the Constitution. So slavery should be permitted in new territories. In 1820, Congress agreed to the Missouri Compromise, which banned slavery in the northern half of the new territories.

The compromise, however, did not hold. In the Kansas

territory, white settlers from the North and the South clashed in bloody battles over whether the land should be open to slavery. In Congress, a southern Congressman attacked a northern senator in the Senate, beating him with a cane until he collapsed, bloodied and unconscious. With passions so high, many Americans looked to the Supreme Court to solve the slavery issue. That opportunity appeared in 1857 in a case filed by a slave named Dred Scott.

The Dred Scott Decision

In 1834, Dred Scott traveled with his white owner from Missouri, then a slave state, to Illinois, a free state. Two years later, Scott and his owner moved to the Wisconsin territory, which was not a state at all. According to the Missouri Compromise, slavery was not permitted in the Wisconsin territory.

By 1842, Dred Scott and his wife, Harriet, were back in St. Louis, Missouri, and in 1846 they asked a court for their freedom. The Scotts claimed that they had been held as slaves both in a state, Illinois, and a territory, Wisconsin, where slavery was against the law. After several

Dred Scott, a slave, took his fight for freedom to the Supreme Court.

29

Chief Justice Roger Taney announced the Court's decision that a slave was not a citizen and had no rights.

years of legal arguments, the case ended up before the Supreme Court.

The case raised enormous questions. These questions were threatening to tear the nation apart. Which state law should be obeyed? The territory question was even more explosive, since the territories were under Congressional law. According to the Missouri Compromise, slavery was illegal in the Wisconsin territory. Was the Congress for or against slavery? Did, Dred Scott, a slave, have any rights at all?

Understanding the importance of the case, many Americans waited nervously for the Court's decision. On March 6, 1857, Chief Justice Roger Taney read the decision of the Court before a chamber filled with journalists, leaders, and common citizens. In a whispery voice, Taney said that Scott was still a slave, because slavery was the law of the United States. Congress had no right to exclude slavery from the territories. The Missouri Compromise, according to Taney, was illegal. Taney, who himself had owned slaves, further wrote that slaves and even free black people had no rights whatsoever. The founders, wrote Taney, did not include them as citizens when they wrote the Declaration of Independence. Since Scott was not a citizen, he had no right to file a suit in the first place.

It was a sweeping decision that left observers stunned. Taney did not just settle the question of Dred Scott. He said that all American men were created equal, unless they were black. He tried to solve the debate over slavery once and for all.

Taney's effort, however, failed miserably. Critics attacked the decision because it ignored the historical fact that black people in some states had been citizens for decades. Abraham Lincoln, who became famous for making speeches against slavery, asked what had happened to the Declaration of Independence, famous for its phrase that "all men are created equal"? Should it be rewritten to say, "except for people with dark skin"? If one race was excluded, why not others? Lincoln pointed out that the founders were all English. Should the Declaration of Independence say, "all men are created equal, except the Irish, Germans, and the Scottish"?

Northern newspapers published articles attacking the decision, and angry crowds held rallies in northern cities. The relationship between the North and South was poisoned even further. Three years after the decision, the country broke apart in open, bloody Civil War.

The reputation of the Supreme Court was shattered by the

Within three years of the Dred Scott decision, the United States became involved in a civil war. This illustration depicts the battle at Antietam between Northern and Southern troops.

decision. After the Civil War began, Taney wrote to President Lincoln, protesting Lincoln's war actions. Lincoln ignored him.

Taney's death in 1864 showed how low the Supreme Court's popularity had fallen. Taney "earned the gratitude of his country at last by dying," wrote an observer. "Better late than never." A chief justice later called the Dred Scott decision the Supreme Court's "self inflicted wound."

Dred Scott, however, did not live long enough to see the Civil War. After the decision, he was returned to his original owners, who freed him and his family in May 1857. Scott died a year later of tuberculosis and was buried in St. Louis.

Plessy v. *Ferguson*

In the early 1860s, the Court moved into new quarters. The front bench, where the judges sat, was raised. Elegant marble pillars framed the chamber. More importantly, the judges finally had a separate room where they could put on their robes. The court opened when the judges walked through parted velvet curtains and took their seats on the bench. A marshal announced, "God save the United States and this Honorable Court" when they entered. This announcement is still used today.

After the Civil War ended in 1865, Congress passed three amendments to the Constitution, the first new amendments in sixty years. The Thirteenth, Fourteenth, and Fifteenth Amendments effectively overturned the Dred Scott decision. They declared slavery illegal, made all people citizens, and protected the voting rights of the newly freed male slaves. The Supreme Court, however, made several crucial decisions that undermined the amendments. One of the most important was a case called *Plessy* v. *Ferguson*.

In 1892, a man named Homer Plessy bought a first-class train ticket in New Orleans, Louisiana. Plessy, who had one black great-grandparent, sat in a train car reserved for whites. When Plessy refused to leave, a police officer was called and Plessy was arrested.

Supreme Court Justice Henry B. Brown wrote the majority opinion of the justices' decision in Plessy v. Ferguson, *stating that segregation was legal as long as the conditions were equal for each race.*

Plessy hoped to challenge a Louisiana segregation law. At court, Plessy's lawyers argued that being forced to sit in a separate car violated the Thirteen and Fourteenth Amendments. Being sent to a separate train car was a humiliating reminder to black people that they had once been slaves.

On May 18, 1896, however, the justices ruled against Plessy. Justice Henry B. Brown wrote the opinion. Brown noted that the object of the Fourteenth Amendment "was undoubtedly to enforce the absolute equality of the two races before the law." Brown then claimed, however, that separating people according to their race was not discrimination as long as both races enjoyed equal conditions. If black train riders felt offended by sitting in a separate car, wrote Brown, it was because they chose to see it that way.

Not every justice agreed. Justice John Marshall Harlan wrote an angry dissent. "Our Constitution is colorblind, and neither knows nor tolerates classes among citizens. In respect of civil rights, all citizens are equal before the law,'" he wrote. "The thin disguise of 'equal' accommodations for passengers in railroad coaches will not mislead anyone, nor atone for the wrong this day done."

The *Plessy* case made discrimination against African-Americans legal. The decision shows that Supreme Court justices are simply people who often share the views of other Americans. Most white Americans at that time, especially in the South, did not consider African-Americans to be their equals. Neither did most of the justices on the Supreme Court. That view, however, would change with time. Old justices died or retired and were replaced. New justices, appointed by different presidents, brought new ideas and attitudes to the Court.

The Supreme Court and the Civil Rights Movement

For sixty years after the *Plessy* decision, African-Americans battled against the laws and customs that kept them from the jobs, education, and homes that many Americans enjoyed. In the 1950s, African-Americans finally began to win cases in court. The Supreme Court's landmark decision in *Brown* v. *Board of Education*, described at the

John Marshall Harlan

John Marshall Harlan's father served in Congress, and he was so awed by John Marshall that he named his son after him. Harlan, of course, went on to write the famous dissent in the *Plessy* case. Harlan's grandson was named after *him*—John Marshall Harlan (pictured above). He also served as a justice on the Supreme Court, from 1955 to 1971.

Thurgood Marshall (center) argued against school segregation in front of the Supreme Court during Brown v. Board of Education. *He later became a Supreme Court justice.*

opening of this book, was just the beginning. In the years following the *Brown* case, the Court struck down laws that prevented African-Americans from getting equal jobs, from getting equal education, and from voting.

The Court at that time was lead by a justice named Earl Warren. Warren had been governor of California. With his experience in politics, Warren was able to convince other justices to make enormously important decisions.

It was an extraordinary time. The country remained divided as African-Americans and their supporters demanded equal rights. The Supreme Court, however, made the forceful decisions that Congress and the president could not make. In that role, it extended the protections of the Bill of Rights to all Americans. The Supreme Court, through its decisions, demanded that the United States live up to its ideals. "The highest court in the land, the guardian of our national conscience," read a *New York Times* editorial on May 18, 1954, "has reaffirmed its faith—and the undying American faith—in the equality of all men and all children before the law." As one commentator later said, "Thank God for the Supreme Court."

Not everyone, however, agreed. The Court did not just strike down segregation. In the 1960s and 1970s, the Court ordered school children to be bused to other schools, simply to mix students of different races. The result was often chaos. Some believed the Court had stepped outside its bounds. The Court was supposed to review law, they argued, not tell people how to live their lives.

The decision in Brown v. Board of Education *meant that school segregation was illegal. Unfortunately, many African-American students faced harassment when they went to white schools.*

The Bill of Rights was designed to protect personal rights and freedoms, such as the right to a speedy trial soon after arrest, freedom of speech, and freedom of religion.

Chapter Five

Freedom of . . .

Since it was founded, the Supreme Court has decided many important cases about the government, the law, and the rights of corporations. In the 1900s, however, the most important decisions have concerned individual rights, such as the right to speak, to write, to worship, or to go to court, without interference from the government. The Court interpreted the Bill of Rights as applying to all citizens. In decision after decision, the Court struck down federal and state laws. In this role, the Court became the guardian of the rights of each and every American.

Students recite the Pledge of Allegiance in their classroom. The Gobitas family objected to this practice because of their religious beliefs and took their case to the Supreme Court.

Freedom of Religion

In October 1935, two schoolchildren in Minersville, Pennsylvania, did something very controversial. They refused to salute the American flag and say the Pledge of Allegiance. Lillian and William Gobitas were members of the Jehovah's Witnesses, a religious group that objects to saluting anything but God. The superintendent and the school board, however, expelled Lillian and William at their next meeting. The children's father, Walter Gobitas, promised, "I'm going to take you to court for this!"

Walter kept his word. The case went all the way to the Supreme Court and was heard on April 25, 1940. By that time, World War II had started in Europe and was threatening the United States. Justice Felix Frankfurter, an immigrant from Austria, argued to the other justices that children should be forced to recite the pledge. He spoke passionately about "the role of the public school in instilling love of country."

The pledge, he argued, was only concerned with government, not with religion. The other justices were convinced. In his opinion, Frankfurter wrote that "we live by symbols," and the flag "is a symbol of our national unity." Laws that made children salute the flag in school were constitutional.

That decision, however, only stood for three years. The other justices soon began having second thoughts about the issue. When another flag salute case came before the Court, the justices decided differently. Justice Robert Jackson wrote in the opinion that each citizen enjoys **fundamental rights**, rights that cannot be taken away by law or by elected government officials. One of these rights is the freedom of religion. These rights "depend on the outcome of no elections," wrote Jackson. Jehovah's Witnesses were free to return to public school without needing to salute the flag. To make its point clear, the Court issued the decision on June 14, 1943, Flag Day.

Freedom of Speech and the Right to a Free Press

In 1917, the United States entered World War I against Germany. A wave of patriotism swept through the United States. German words used in English were renamed. "Sauerkraut," for example, was changed to "liberty cabbage." Congress also passed the Espionage Act, which made it a crime to criticize the government.

Many people in the United States, however, openly protested against the war. They didn't see the point in fighting, and they printed their views in pamphlets and newspapers. Others simply said that the government was wrong. In the tense war atmosphere, many of these people were arrested. A Montana rancher, who remarked in a saloon that "the

The Highest Court in the Land

The Supreme Court moved into its current building in 1935, leaving the chamber in the basement of the Capitol. On the top floor of the building is a basketball court. Court workers jokingly call it the "highest court in the land."

United States was only fighting for Wall Street Millionaires," was thrown in jail.

Did the Espionage Act violate freedom of speech, as protected by the First Amendment of the Bill of Rights? At first, the Supreme Court answered no. Not all speech is protected. Justice Oliver Wendell Holmes wrote that you could not shout "Fire!" in a crowded theater if there was no fire. People might panic and rush to the exits, leading to injuries and deaths. Holmes further argued that the government may restrict free speech when facing a "clear and present danger." World War I was a clear danger, he said.

After the war ended, Americans became nervous about **communists**, a political group that advocated radical change

in the government. Communists also argued that people should give up their ownership of property to a central state. This was considered a very dangerous idea that pitted rich against poor. Even more alarming, some communists urged the use of violence to achieve their goals. The patriotism of World War I was replaced by a "Red Scare," so-named because many communists used the color red as their symbol. A young woman, Anita Whitney, who was a member of the American Communist Party, was arrested and convicted under California's Criminal Syndicalism Act in 1920 of belonging to a party advocating unlawful violence to accomplish political change. In 1927, the Supreme Court upheld the conviction.

Oliver Wendell Holmes wrote in his opinion that not all speech is protected by the First Amendment.

This time, however, Justice Holmes and Justice Louis Brandeis, dissented. "Men feared witches and burnt women," wrote Brandeis. "It is the function of speech to free men from the bonds of irrational fears." Holmes supported Brandeis. Whitney was not a "clear and present danger," he wrote. Though the other justices did not agree with Brandeis and Holmes, lawyers and citizens would later use their dissents to question and demand more protection for free speech.

That chance came in 1960, when a southern police commissioner named L. B. Sullivan sued the newspaper, *The New*

Justice Louis Brandeis (front row, first person on the right) objected to the majority opinion against Anita Whitney's case.

York Times. Sullivan was angered by an advertisement that ran in the paper. The advertisement called attention to protests in the South against segregation. Even though Sullivan was not named in the advertisement, his policemen were criticized.

Sullivan (second from left) sued The New York Times *for libel and won in a lower court, but the Supreme Court overturned the earlier decision.*

Important Supreme Court Decisions

Gideon v. Wainwright (1963)

In 1961, Clarence Earl Gideon was arrested and charged with breaking into a pool room in Panama City, Florida. Gideon was poor, and the Florida court denied him a state lawyer. Gideon was sentenced to five years. Gideon wrote a letter to the Supreme Court, which heard his case and ruled that the state must provide poor defendants with a lawyer.

Miranda v. Arizona (1966)

In this decision, the Supreme Court ruled that police have to read each suspect his or her "rights." That's why, when arresting someone, police must now say, "You have the right to remain silent. Anything you say can and will be used against you in a court of law. You have the right to speak to an attorney, and to have an attorney present during any questioning. If you cannot afford a lawyer, one will be provided for you at government expense."

Claiming that he had been **defamed**, Sullivan sued in a state court and won $500,000. The case was appealed to the Supreme Court.

Was *The New York Times* protected by free speech? This time, the Supreme Court answered yes. Justice William Brennan wrote that criticisms "and sometimes unpleasantly sharp attacks against public officials" were protected in American society. With this decision, the Supreme Court made the right to speech and a free press in the United States among the strongest in the world.

This is where the Supreme Court justices hear arguments.

Chapter Six

The Court Today

Today, thousands of cases are appealed to the Court, but the Court only has time to hear a few of them. The justices choose important cases that raise new questions about the law. When a Supreme Court case is heard, the justices listen to **oral arguments**. Each side gets thirty minutes to argue their case. The justices pepper the lawyers with questions designed to reveal more about their position, its weaknesses, and its strengths. Sometimes, the justices get impatient with

47

the answers. "You say maybe yes, maybe no, you just don't know," one justice told a lawyer.

Normally, no news organization is allowed to broadcast oral arguments. However, in 2000, the Court decided to allow it. An extraordinary case had come before the Court, and the entire country wanted to hear the arguments. The Court's decision would determine the next president of the United States.

Gore v. *Bush*

November 11, 2000, was Election Day. Millions of Americans went to the polls to elect representatives and a new president. The presidential race, between Al Gore and George W. Bush,

Determining the winner of the 2000 presidential election turned into a difficult legal battle. Here, an official is recounting votes cast in Florida while representatives look on.

was extremely close. Midnight came and passed, but the votes were still being counted. Only thousands of votes separated the two candidates.

By November 12, no one was sure who had won. Gore admitted defeat, but then called Bush and said it was too close to call. Attention soon settled on Florida, a crucial state that Bush won by only 2,000 votes. When Gore asked for a recount, the Florida state courts agreed. Inspectors were sent to examine the voting sheets and determine the exact tally.

Bush, however, asked the Supreme Court to stop the recount, saying that the Florida courts had ruled improperly. The Supreme Court agreed to hear the case and have arguments broadcast live on radio, for the first time in the Court's history. On December 12, the Court announced its decision. By a vote of 5 to 4, the Court ordered the count to be halted, effectively making George W. Bush president.

The Court's decision brought it an uncomfortable amount of attention. While some supported the Court, others openly questioned whether or not the nine justices had the power to make such a crucial decision. Some attacked the reasoning

The legal fight over the recounting of votes in Florida went all the way to the Supreme Court, which decided to halt the recount efforts.

A Tight Schedule

The Supreme Court's schedule begins on the first Monday in October and lasts through the year until summer recess. The Court considers an enormous number of cases, more than seven thousand in the 1999–2000 session alone. This reflects a large increase, considering the Court handled 2,313 cases in 1960. Of these seven thousand cases, the Court selected only eighty for oral arguments. The Court's written opinions total more than 5,000 pages. More than four hundred court employees are needed to keep the process flowing smoothly.

behind the opinion, calling it poor and unconvincing. As Marshall had long ago recognized, the Court also looked weak because the decision was only supported by five of the justices. The other four justices wrote angry dissents.

The *Bush* v. *Gore* decision damaged the Court's reputation. The justices were supposed to be above politics, but many citizens believed the justices voted for Bush because they supported his political party. Even years after Bush settled in the White House, many people refuse to call him "president."

A Continuing Role

Despite the Bush–Gore controversy, the Supreme Court remains secure as the nation's highest interpreter of the law and the guardian of the Constitution. The Court has also become more diverse. Throughout the Court's history, virtually all Supreme Court justices have been white men. Thurgood Marshall, a legendary civil rights lawyer, was named to the Court by President Lyndon Johnson in 1967. He was the first African-American justice.

In 1981, Sandra Day O'Connor was appointed the first female justice in 1981 by President Ronald Reagan. A graduate of Stanford Law School, O'Connor created a career in law at a time when few men would accept women lawyers. In 1993, O'Connor was joined by another female justice, Ruth Bader Ginsburg.

These judges will face difficult decisions in the future. American society is always changing. New disputes, perhaps over national security, perhaps over human cloning, may find their way to the Supreme Court.

Thankfully, the Court will be there. Though many people have criticized the Court, no one challenges its power or importance in American society. It is safe to say that the Court will play this role as long as the Constitution exists.

"The Court had only the power to persuade," wrote journalist Anthony Lewis. "But that has proved enough to defeat presidents and Congresses, enough to give the Supreme Court the last word in much of American life."

Sandra Day O'Connor was the first woman appointed to the Supreme Court.

Timeline

1787	The Continental Congress meets in Philadelphia and establishes a "supreme Court" in Article III of the Constitution.
1789	Congress passes the Judiciary Act, which created a Supreme Court of six judges with one chief justice and five associate justices.
1790	The Supreme Court holds its first session in New York City.
1801	John Marshall becomes chief justice of the Supreme Court. Congress passes another judiciary act, which created new federal court positions.
1803	The Supreme Court decides in *Marbury* v. *Madison* that the Congress did not have the right to give or take power from the Supreme Court and declares that the Judiciary Act of 1801 is unconstitutional.
1819	In *McCulloch* v. *Maryland,* the Supreme Court decides that the federal government has the right to establish a national bank, but the states cannot tax federal institutions.
1835	Chief Justice John Marshall dies.
1857	The Supreme Court decides that Dred Scott, a slave, is not a citizen of the United States.
1896	The Supreme Court rules against Homer Plessy, an African-American who sued to challenge segregation laws in the *Plessy* v. *Ferguson* case. The Court decides that separating people according to their race was not discrimination as long as both races had equal accomodations.

1943	The Court decides that Jehovah's Witnesses can attend public school without saluting the flag because of their right to freedom of religion.
1954	The Supreme Court announces its decision regarding *Brown v. Board of Education* on May 17, declaring school segregation illegal.
1963	In *Gideon v. Wainwright*, the Court decides that states must provide poor defendants with a lawyer.
1966	In *Miranda v. Arizona*, the Court rules that the police must inform each suspect of his or her rights.
2000	The Supreme Court hears arguments regarding the recount of votes in Florida in the 2000 presidential election in *Bush v. Gore*. The Court orders the recount stopped.

Glossary

abolish—to do away with or put an end to

agricultural—farming

appeal—a legal party's request for a higher court to review the decision of a lower court

checks and balances—these are the powers each branch of the American government can exercise over the other. The intention is to prevent any one branch from getting too strong.

communists—people who support a political belief system that promotes collective ownership of property

Constitutional Convention—this is the group that met in the summer of 1787 to reform the Articles of Confederation. The convention drafted the Constitution. It has also been called the Federal Convention or the Philadelphia Convention.

defamed—having one's character or standing incorrectly attacked in public

dissenting opinion—a justice's expression of disagreement with a majority Court decision

fundamental rights—rights defined by the Court as being unalterable, especially by new laws or elected officials

judiciary—the system of courts

lawsuit—an argument or dispute brought before a court

majority—when more than half the justices support a decision, which then becomes the will of the Court

opinion—a formal expression of a Supreme Court decision

oral arguments—this is the process in which lawyers go before the courts and argue their case. Judges can also use the time to ask the lawyers to explain their position.

precedent—a decision made by the Court that becomes an example to be applied by other courts in similar cases

segregation—a system of laws in the United States that separated white and black people

unanimously—everyone deciding the same thing, with total agreement

unconstitutional—a Court ruling that means a law does not agree with the Constitution

To Find Out More

Books

Hall, Kermit L. *The Oxford Guide to United States Supreme Court Decisions.* New York: Oxford University Press, 1999.

Irons, Peter. *A People's History of the Supreme Court.* New York: Penguin Books, 1999.

Irons, Peter (ed.). *May It Please the Court: Courts, Kids, and the Constitution.* New York: New Press, 2000.

McElroy, Lisa Tucker. *Meet My Grandmother: She's a Supreme Court Justice.* Brookfield, CT: Millbrook Press, 2000.

Patrick, John J. *The Supreme Court of the United States: A Student Companion.* New York: Oxford University Press Children's Books, 2002.

Rakove, Jack. *Original Meanings: Politics and Ideas in the Making of the Constitution.* New York: Vintage Books, 1997.

Raskin, Jamin B. *We the Students: Supreme Court Decisions for and About Students.* Washington: Congressional Quarterly Books, 2003.

Organizations and Online Sites

Dred Scott Case: The Supreme Court Decision
http://www.pbs.org/wgbh/aia/part4/4h2933.html
This Web page is devoted to the Dred Scott decision.

Landmark Supreme Court Cases
http://www.landmarkcases.org/
This excellent site lists important Supreme Court cases, their opinions, and summaries of their importance.

The Rise and Fall of Jim Crow
http://www.pbs.org/wnet/jimcrow/index.html
This is the Web site for the PBS program on Jim Crow—the laws that segregated black and white in the South after the Civil War.

The Supreme Court Historical Society

http://www.supremecourthistory.org/

This site is devoted to Supreme Court history. It includes biographical sketches of each Supreme Court justice and special features on Court controversies.

Supreme Court of the United States

http://www.supremecourtus.gov/

This is the official site for the Supreme Court. It contains background information on the Court, as well as published opinions and upcoming cases.

A Note on Sources

For a general history of the Supreme Court, I relied upon Bernard Schwartz's *A History of the Supreme Court*, Peter Irons's *A People's History of the Supreme Court*, and Kermit L. Hall's *The Oxford Guide to the Supreme Court of the United States*. I found the volumes to be readable, packed with information, and excellent sources of how the Court has changed over the past two hundred years. For a discussion of how the Court was written into the Constitution, I read Jack Rakove's *Original Meanings: Politics and Ideas in the Making of the Constitution*. For studies of individual cases, I read Anthony Lewis's superb books, *Make No Law* and *Gideon's Trumpet*. General information on the Court and how it works today can be found on the Supreme Court's Web site.

—*Brendan January*

Index

Numbers in *italics* indicate illustrations.

About the Author

Brendan January is an award-winning author of more than twenty-five books for young readers. A graduate of Haverford College and Columbia Graduate School of Journalism, January has written for the *Philadelphia Inquirer* and *The Record*. He is a Fulbright Scholar and currently lives in northern New Jersey with his wife and daughter.